LOVE

AND

WAR

The Human Side of Business

THE TALE OF THE ARABIC CHANNEL

BY MARGUERITE M. MOORE

To Ernie Fazio, Merry Nachemin,
Shoshi Bacon and Rosa Venegas
without whose encouragement and support
this book may not have been written.

TABLE OF CONTENTS

FOREWORD

Getting involved with creating a business can be extremely rewarding and frustrating at the same time. I wanted to write this book so my students in entrepreneurship could get a better feel for what it is like to establish a business and to realize that no matter how well you plan and research, there are still things you may have overlooked or did not contemplate at the outset of your journey. As an American, the aspects of doing business with another culture were eye opening. The impact on family life and the expectations and will of an aggressive partner can take a toll and stretch your patience to the limit.

You have no control over the events in the world that may have an effect on your business. I have attempted to illustrate this in the pages of this book.

I realized in thinking about my experiences that there is a story here that would be appealing and interesting to relate to others, and so I created this book for a wider audience than just my aspiring entrepreneur students. I have told this story as I have seen it and experienced it. The impressions that cofounding this business have left me with have helped me grow into a stronger and wiser businessperson.

I hope that you will enjoy and learn from reading this book.

CHAPTER 1

Getting Started

One day in the summer of 1990 my husband, Gamil, came home from work and told me he had a great idea for a business. His stint at being a stockbroker was not going well since the market was in bad shape at that time and there was talk that his brokerage firm would close. He expected that he would be leaving the firm in about two months. He was thinking about doing something that he had envisioned for a long time. And now was the time.

Gamil told me about his idea of opening a television station in New York. He told me it would be targeted at the Arabic population which was growing at that time, and he wanted to do something good for his people. There were many Arabic people moving into New York, especially into Bay Ridge, Brooklyn and Astoria, Queens. Numerous retail stores were opening to cater to them not only in foods but also in clothing. Islamic schools were being established in Brooklyn and Queens, and more and more mosques were opening up in basements and storefronts. Gamil knew about the need for immigrants to have their own foods and be able to be entertained in the evenings at home with their families with good television programs. He knew from experience; he had immigrated to the United States from Egypt in 1978.

I met this news, not with surprise and apprehension, but with the eyes of an investment banker envisioning an opportunity. I had been working at Lehman Brothers as a vice president for many years, and I had learned how to recognize a promising business idea. Putting my banker's hat on I immediately thought about the feasibility of this idea, and asked "Is there a market for Arabic television?" As an American, I wasn't certain of this need. "How many people are there within a certain area and would it be worthwhile to target them? How would we reach them? Where would we get the programming from, and are there any Arabic television stations in the United States at this time?"

I asked Gamil these questions, and he responded positively. I realized in later years that he spoke on instinct or from the gut: he hadn't done any research or inspection of the market need. This would have to be done later. With regard to programming, he would have to find the contacts in Cairo, the Hollywood of the Middle East, who would have the authority to license films and soaps to us in the New York area. Starting a station was another question; it would require money, programming and a location.

Lehman Brothers had an entertainment specialization in its investment bank, and I had access to these bankers. I told Gamil that I would get additional information as to how to start a television station and would let him know of my findings.

Upon arriving at my office the next morning, I phoned Louis Bellemy, a vice president in the media and entertainment group, and asked if we could meet for lunch, and he agreed. At lunch I told him what we were planning on doing and asked him how to go about starting a television station. He replied that there were three ways to get on the air. First, you could buy a television station that had a footprint in the area in which your target market was located. That would cost around three million dollars. Finding one for sale and in the targeted area would be very lucky, to say the least. For example, there was a television station in Florida that featured science fiction movies called the Sci Fi Channel started by two entrepreneurs, who owned Home Town Cable in south Florida, which was later purchased by USA Networks for about five million dollars. Of course, we didn't have that kind of money, so was there another way to do it?

The second way was to lease time on a cable station. Many stations fill in their empty time with locally produced programming. But they charged a fee for each program aired. We would have to deliver our canned programs the day before the airing to the cable company, which would broadcast them.

Paying to put programming on the air was not the way I wanted to go. After all, I didn't want the cable station to make all the money. I wanted the cable station to pay me - which was the third way of getting on the air. We would have to make a presentation to a cable company to ask them to take on our programming. They would give us a channel, and we would be responsible for delivering the signal to their distribution center. I asked Louis if an estimated audience of one hundred thousand people was enough to generate fees that would keep the business going and our personal living expenses as well. "Absolutely," he responded, "that is an excellent number". His enthusiasm for our plan to establish this business gave me the motivation to proceed with speed. "Make a presentation to one of the cable companies and see if they will accept you," he said.

Before we could present ourselves to a cable company, we needed to write a business plan. But first, we needed to obtain a lot of information to determine whether our project was feasible or not. And we needed lots of time to gather research on our target market, determine where the Arabic populations resided in the New York area, find out which cable companies served those areas, and write the business plan.

I soon discovered that Gamil did not like a lot of detail. After five years of marriage I hadn't discovered this about him. When I told him we had to do research and write a business plan, he scoffed at the idea. "We don't need it," he said. He just wanted to plow ahead and get the information required for activating his plan. This was our first disagreement in pursuing this adventure.

The following week Gamil had to appear for jury duty. I reminded him that we had to write the business plan and write it in a certain way. He was still obstinate. I had brought home a book called *Pratt's Guide to Venture Capital* which describes the process to start a business and the steps required to set the plan in motion. He seemed interested in it because it was printed. This was more credible than me telling him we needed to write a business plan. These Arab men! He would rather read the book than believe I knew what I was talking about. Though I had an MBA and experience at one of the most prestigious investment banks in the United States, Gamil had put no credence in what I was telling him. He left for jury duty with this book in his briefcase and told me he would read it while waiting to be called.

CHAPTER 2

Down to Business

When Gamil returned from jury duty he was all excited. He had read *Pratt's* and wanted to write the business plan quickly. As a matter of fact, he wanted it completed yesterday! But we just couldn't start writing the business plan; we had to do the market research to determine the competition, if any, and profile the consumers. We went to visit the Public Library on Forty-Second Street and Fifth Avenue to do the research. At that time, there was no access to the Internet; it simply did not exist for public use.

There we were, seated in the dusty, dimly lit hall of the library with our heads together, searching for information about potential competition in the New York area. We went to the library several times to gather information and found the following: There was no direct competition in the area that was running an Arabic television program seven days a week, twenty-four hours a day. The only thing we found was that there was a two hour radio program out of Boston transmitting on Sundays to an audience residing within a fifty mile radius.

This information gave us confidence that there was a need for our television station. Now we had to find out where there was a concentration of Arabic-speaking people residing. And what were they doing now for television entertainment? They would rent movies from mom-and-pop Arabic stores. These stores would be devoted primarily to renting movies or Arabic grocery stores with movie rentals. The rentals were usually of poor quality, scratched or misused by previous renters, or completely unusable. The Arabic people needed an alternate means of entertainment, and that was television, our television.

We searched Arabic newspapers and visited mosques to find out how many people were in the selected areas. You would think that this was easy to do. We asked Arabic newspaper publishers about how many newspapers were printed and sold per week. They couldn't tell us. We asked the imams in the mosques, the Muslim religious leaders, how many people attended the mosques in a given area. We were met with smiling faces and looks of suspicion by all those we visited, were fed ridiculous rhetoric, and came away with no information.

We needed to verifiy the number of Arabic speaking people and recent immigrants to the area. We called the US Census Bureau to find out how many people were within the New York City area. We were told that the 1990 census wasn't completed yet and that the 1980 census didn't have a count broken down by ethnicity. Therefore, the number of Arabic speaking people was almost impossible to determine.

We decided that we would have to drive around areas of Brooklyn and Queens to see where pockets of Arabs were located. That was easy; we just looked for areas where many Arabic people dressed in cultural clothing were walking around, and where there were several Halal butcher shops, grocery stores and hookah cafes. There also were at least three local small Arabic-language newspapers and the *Pyramids* newspaper from Egypt being sold. We tried to estimate the number of people in those areas; we had to make our "best guess" and "count" them ourselves.

Then we needed to find out about cable companies. We searched for the cable companies that served Queens and Brooklyn. We found that Time Warner Cable and its affiliated companies and Cablevision were the only ones. We would have to obtain marketing material from them in order to become familiar with their services and pricing and to know which areas they served. After studying their coverage areas, we determined that their footprints covered the areas where our targeted populations were located.

Once we decided that we had gathered enough information for our business plan, I started writing. We followed an outline which was found in *Pratt's* and used that for our plan. When Gamil could see how the plan was developing, he was so excited that he started to gather more information on his own. To make it more complete, he gathered maps and growth-rate charts for inclusion in the plan. We projected the number of Arabic households that would sign on to the cable service and determined the income levels of the households. We needed to know this to determine whether they would be able to afford cable television and to get as accurate a count as possible for our projections.

One of the sections of a business plan was the financial statements, including a cash-flow statement, an income statement, and a balance sheet projection for three years. Our rationale when developing the income statement was to determine how many Arabs were residing in our target area, and then decide how many households we would be able to capture with our service. We decided that 1 percent of the market would be a good number, and then decided that a growth rate of 10 percent from month to month would be appropriate for the first year's revenue. But how much should we charge and how would we be positioned on the cable companies' program listings -- as a standard program or as a subscriber fee-based program?

To find out the answer to these questions, we looked at ethnic channels that were being offered: the Korean Channel, the Chinese Channel, and the Indian Channel. These were on the Time Warner Cable system, and they were subscriber, fee-based services offered at nine dollars per month. Cablevision had the Russian Channel, targeting the Brighton Beach section in Brooklyn which also charged nine dollars. So we decided to charge the nine dollar fee, the going rate, for our programming. Sometimes you have to take what the competition or comparable companies are getting for their product and live with that, instead of trying to determine what your price will be based on, your expenses and cost structure and then adding on a profit margin.

Then we needed to determine the expenses that we would en-counter in running the business. We looked at annual reports of comparable companies and saw how their expense accounts were portrayed. We then had a list of expenses that were com-mon to these companies. We used those expense accounts and figured out how much we would incur for our small operation, based on our needs.

It took about three months to complete the business plan. I must say that we were both very proud of our project and the information about the culture and habits of the Arabic people contained in it.

CHAPTER 3

Cable Company Solicitations

We were ready to call Cablevision and Time Warner Cable to get an appointment for our presentation. But who should we talk to at those companies? I determined that we call the vice president of programming and the general manager of the cable systems for appointments. We were lucky; we got an appointment with Time Warner Cable first, and mailed our business plan to them for their perusal. Cablevision was not receptive to our plan, since they had no free channel space to offer us at that time.

We met with Steve Pagano, the general manager, and Hugh Pinero, the vice president of marketing. (Pinero later left Time Warner and became the president and CEO of XM Satellite Radio which was later merged into Sirius Satellite Radio). They greeted us warmly, and we made our presentation to them. Well, actually Gamil started, and I filled in and answered questions about the business plan's financials.

They were very interested, and they questioned Gamil on his background and interest in television. He had experience in radio broadcasting in Cairo. He had two radio programs -- one for traditional Arabic music and the other for rock and roll and heavy metal. Gamil remarked at one point during their inquiries, "What do you think? I just parked my camel outside!" I contained my horror at this remark as I almost fell off my chair. However, everyone laughed.

Steve mentioned that they had been approached by several Arabic people for television time, but they didn't get anywhere with them. We were the only ones who approached them in a professional manner and presented a complete business plan. They indicated one thing to us: they wanted us to go back and recast our numbers to reflect a split of 70/30 on the subscription sales. Hmm, 70/30? What did this mean? I stirred up my courage and asked: "Who will get the 70 percent?"

"Why, you will, of course," Steve replied. "We want to help you, you're a start-up."

We quickly revised the financial statements, and Gamil went back to Time Warner to present the recast numbers. Later that day, he called me at work and asked, "Are you sitting down?"

"Why?" I asked.

"Because we have a signed contract with Time Warner!"

Time Warner was one of the three major cable companies at that time, and we little people had a contract with them! In addition to being almost delirious with happiness, all I could think of was, "We have no programming, we have no space, and we have no investors. Oh my, we have to get hopping!"

It was then that our adventure began. We decided that to make more sales and, hopefully, more profit and enjoy economies of scale we had to develop a network that would include additional cable companies and coverage in the area. Once we had the operations of the channel established, we could expand without additional expenditures for operations. Our overhead would be fixed.

We visited other cable companies in our targeted area - U.S. Cable of Paterson, Suburban Cable, Comcast Cablevision of Jersey City – and made presentation to them. Once we told them we had a contract with Time Warner, they all signed with us. No questions asked.

We had our channel on Time Warner, and we had our channels on the other cable companies. All we needed now was money, programming and a location.

CHAPTER 4

Money, Money, Money

Oh, my gosh! Where are we going to get the money?

Well, business literature says that you should first contact friends and relatives for money. Start-ups are not generally funded by loans from banks. I had some money to put into the business, but it would not be enough. I estimated that we needed to raise eight hundred thousand dollars to set up shop. We had to put our thinking caps on. Who do we know? I knew that Lehman Brothers had a Partners' Fund. Gamil had worked at Bear Stearns and knew several of the partners. He also knew a friend who was dating a man who worked for Goldman Sachs.

My inquiry came up empty. It appeared that the Lehman Partners' Fund was only interested in biotechnology and healthcare. Those industries were the "flavor of the month" at that time and were "hot." Gamil had the same results at Bear Stearns. When all seemed dark and we were losing faith, his friend called and said that her boyfriend from Goldman Sachs would like to meet with us.

We were hopeful. It appeared that her friend was part of a group consisting of four individuals who invested in start-ups. We gave him our business plan, and made a date for dinner. After a lengthy dinner with the potential investors we had a deal. They would invest up to half a million dollars, so we had to look for three hundred thousand more.

The Arabic world is very small here. It seems that talk moves like a virus within this community. They love to keep in close contact and tell stories, and the news of an Arabic television station in the area was very exciting. Gamil was approached by an acquaintance, Yousef, who had a partner who sold rights to films and soap operas from Cairo. Yousef had a wedding and event photography business. They expressed an interest in providing films, entertainment, and soap operas in exchange for a share of the television company. Terrific! This would eliminate some of the money we had to raise, but we still needed more.

Along came a real estate broker of Arabic descent and his business associate, an accountant, who were very interested in investing. I guess being an owner of a television station is sexy. They would provide an additional eighty thousand dollars. Gamil was excited and said we were ready to see our attorneys and make a deal. I would give him fifty thousand dollars for a percentage of the business.

Our attorneys recommended a limited partnership form of business, with Gamil the general partner and the others the limited (or silent) partners. After several drafts of the partnership agreement and much haggling, we had a final document. We closed and signed the partnership agreement and collected the money in December 1990.

In the meantime, Time Warner was pressuring us to start our television station. They wanted us to be on the air by April 1991. "Get your location by the end of the week," Steve told Gamil. "We want to start your programming." I reminded Gamil that we did not reach our goal of eight hundred thousand dollars, and that we would be short of funds right after establishing the business. But he replied, "I promised Steve that we would start by April 8. We have to do this." By his own sheer will, he would open on that date; he would do it or be damned.

CHAPTER 5

Finding a Location

All the management and business books I've read indicate that one has to be aware of the environmental effects of the world on your business. Effects like economic, political and legal, technological, nature, competition, social/demographic, can make or break your business since you have no control over them. Business owners have to watch the papers and listen to news analysts' reports for word on happenings and events that could affect their ability to make sales. One such uncontrollable event happened to us while we were looking for space – the beginning of the First Iraq War.

I first heard of the news of the bombing of Iraq and our troops infiltrating there on the radio while I was driving down Sepulveda Blvd in Los Angeles while on a business trip for Lehman. I pulled into a gas station to listen to the news. I was shocked and wondered how this event would affect our being able to open the business. I called Gamil in New York and asked him if he had heard the news. "Yes," he replied, "I don't believe that it will be harmful to our efforts." I remember sitting down with him at home later and watching CNN and the live reports of the bombing. It was incredible to watch history in the making. We were glued to the television set in the evenings to keep up with the news. This event made CNN a well-respected news company.

In January and February 1991, Gamil commenced a whirlwind search for space. He went to Exchange Place in Jersey City, where there were many spaces for lease on good terms. One building management asked what kind of business he was in; he replied, "An Arabic television station." Once he said that magic word *Arabic*, they wanted nothing to do with him. He went to many locations around the city with the same result.

But Gamil would not be defeated. He was determined to find space; he had committed to Time Warner to start by April 8. He finally went to Exchange Place in Lower Manhattan, one block south of Wall Street. At that time, Lower Manhattan was a veritable ghost town and in a depression. Landlords had many tenants moving uptown to nicer quarters, leaving many buildings vacant or nearly vacant. This was the case with 20 Exchange Place; buildings were partially occupied. Ironically, I had worked for a law firm at 20 Exchange when I was in my twenties. It was a grand, art deco building and was once the headquarters of First National City Bank, later Citibank. It was strange to learn that these buildings were no longer in favor.

Gamil met with the building manager, who showed him space on one of the upper floors and he said he would build a small studio, editing room, and three offices as long as we would take a ten-year lease. We would not have to pay for the renovations, and the first rent payment would be due in six months. So this was a savings for us. The lease payments were very reasonable, and we asked for the lease agreement. Our attorneys reviewed it, and we were ready to sign on.

We agreed with the building management that we would not advertise that we were an Arabic television station, and the signage in the directory in the building lobby would refer to our partnership name and not the name of our station: The Arabic Channel. Our

Arabic ethnicity was not an issue as long as we didn't promote the fact. We were very concerned that with the bombing of Baghdad, there might be retaliation if people knew that there was an Arabic television station right in the heart of the Wall Street business district.

CHAPTER 6

Building a Network

Distribution was critical to our business. We had to distribute our signal to Time Warner's main distribution hub in Manhattan, to US Cable of Patterson, New Jersey and to Comcast Cablevision of Jersey City. The cable companies would then transmit our signal to their subscribers of our channel. There would be three connections to cities near and far. But how could we transmit our signal to them? We couldn't deliver tapes to each cable company by bicycle every day. We had to connect all three with our programming and build a network.

We discovered that the only feasible way at that time was to use microwave transmission. With microwave, we could transmit from the roof of Exchange Place to Patterson and to Red Hook in Brooklyn for Time Warner. Jersey City was a short distance so that could be done from our office. Large microwave dishes had to be installed for Red Hook, Brooklyn, and Patterson on the roof of the building, and a smaller one in our office. Another set of microwave dishes had to be installed at each receiving point in the three locations. Microwave was favorable because bad weather didn't affect the transmissions since it transmitted in a concentrated, narrow beam to the target destination. It provided a clear and sharp picture for our viewers. We had to pay rent for the roof space occupied by these dishes and pay for the monthly transmission fee. But we had not fully anticipated that in our projections.

The day for the installation of the dishes arrived. Two large dishes were to be installed on the roof of the building – fifty-five floors above the street and installed on towers on the roof. It was a sunny, windy, and cold day in late March. I certainly wouldn't want to go up to the roof and work on those dishes; the wind was cutting and cold so high up. But Gamil was running up and down to the roof and back to the office to check on the progress. Cables had to be lowered from the dishes on the roof through the elevator shafts into our offices on the forty-fifth floor and connected to the broadcast station. One of the elevators had to be taken out of service that day. It was a dangerous and delicate installation because of the length of the cables being lowered in the elevator shaft and the confined space that the installers had to contend with, but it was done by the end of the day.

While workers were installing the microwave dishes on the roof, the broadcast equipment was being installed in our premises. We had a beautiful television station and office, and one of Gamil's friends was a Panasonic engineer who installed the broadcast equipment: switchers, players and recorders. We also had gotten an editing suite and switchers -- the machines that enabled the editing of film-- that Time Warner was disposing of. The installation of the broadcast equipment and editing suite occurred simultaneously with the installation of the microwave dishes. It took hours, and the men worked into the next day on the broadcast to get it all done. After all, we had just five days to be up and on the air.

When the installation was complete, we tested the system and then ran some programming through. All three locations received our clear signal simultaneously. We were ready! Happy day! We had a network!

We had to hire five employees to help run the station. Gamil looked among the Arabic community for people who could operate television cameras and do editing. We also needed a person who could read the news, and we needed people with good voices and good Arabic who could do voice-overs. Many people came to our office, but only a few were selected. Gamil chose those who had experience in television in Egypt or had experience in camera work. Of course, I was concerned that these people had working papers, Green cards; Social Security numbers and that they were able to do what they said they could do. I didn't want Immigration to fine the station.

I soon realized that the people Gamil had hired were not the best people he could have chosen. We discovered that one of them could not read English. I guess because we were an Arabic station he felt he could get away without having to read or speak English well. I'm sure you have read some management books or heard that you are only as good as the people you hire. And, if you have weaknesses, you should hire people competent enough to offset those weaknesses. I realized that several people were not good enough to hold their own at their jobs. I suggested to Gamil that he fire them and find other, more qualified people by testing them. He indicated that he knew this and was reluctant to fire them. But he preferred to change their schedules from week to week and push them so that they would leave on their own. This did happen with all but one person who is still with us today. I still believe that this person holds Gamil back from excelling and bringing The Arabic Channel to a higher level.

I also realized that Gamil needed to be in control. He never hired people who were better qualified and smarter than he was because he may not be able to control them. So we were left with people he needed to supervise for them to perform their tasks correctly and get things done.

As the head of the business, Gamil's responsibilities were to develop new business. Instead, he edited because he was the one who could do it the best. When his partners realized this they told him that he should never go into the editing room and should spend his time seeking new clients and expanding the network.

CHAPTER 7

The Launch

About a month before we opened the station to viewers, Gamil came home quite upset. He had found a flyer on our car that said someone was starting a television program soon and that further information would be forthcoming. There would be competition right on our coattails. I looked at the flyer and said, "It doesn't appear it will be a full-blown television station. And, look at it this way: these people, whoever they are, are advertising for you." He thought about it and realized that it could be true that they were doing our initial advertising for us and making the community aware of the advent of Arabic television.

However, we needed to let people know on our own that The Arabic Channel would be starting on April 8 and on three systems. We placed an ad in the Arabic newspaper with the largest distribution in the region, *Al Alewaa*. We provided contact numbers so people could order the channel. The three cable companies would offer two weeks of free service. We would collect the names and addresses of people who wanted the service and then send that information to the cable companies for installation.

Opening day came, and we were so excited to launch the station. The partners of the company came to the station to witness the launch and to drink to its success. An exhausted Gamil went "live" to make an announcement about the station, and then we went to our programming lineup. We were the first Arabic television station in the United States operating twenty-four hours a day, seven days a week. It was quite an accomplishment, and a gift to the Arabic people.

The phones went crazy; people called with congratulations and wished us success. Flowers and plants filled the office. Many called to order the service. As soon as we put the phone down, another call came in. We had five lines, and we were going crazy answering them. We needed to take the calls, because the cable companies did not have Arabic-speaking personnel to do it. We were afraid that if no one could help them by speaking Arabic, we would lose the order.

I remember a funny call I took from a fellow who had just arrived from Egypt the day before and wanted the television service. He gave me his name in broken English. Then I asked for his address. He said that he lived above the pharmacy near the corner of Sixty-eighth Street and Third Avenue in Brooklyn. In their native land this is how Arabs would pass on their addresses for deliveries or for friends who might visit.

"That is great!" I said. "What is the building number?"

"Building number?" he replied. I asked that he go downstairs and outside, and look at the building, probably above the door, and call me back with the building number.

We compiled the list of names and addresses and sent them to the cable companies. In the first week, we had five hundred requests for service. If we kept going at that rate for the next few weeks, we would exceed our projections.

Each day at around 1:00 p.m. and again at 5:00 p.m., the male workers, including Gamil, stopped work and threw down their Muslim prayer rugs and prayed facing East for about five minutes.

No phone calls could be taken during the prayer sessions, and one of the women had to watch the broadcast in case there was a problem with one of the tapes. The company had the flexibility to allow for the religious practices and observances of its employees. This was interesting to me: at home Gamil did not pray daily but on occasion, and now he was practicing daily prayer. I assumed he was grateful to God that he had a television station and was giving thanks. As time progressed he was becoming more and more religious, keeping the holidays and going to Friday prayer.

When I had a day off from Lehman Brothers or a holiday, I went to the station to help out.   One day, the phone rang and no one picked it up. So I did. Using my broken Arabic, I tried to help the Arabic person on the line, who was inquiring about something. I tried to help him as best I good. He suddenly asked in English, "Are you an American?"

"Yes", I responded.

"Then why are you working there? You are not Arabic."

Really! I am just one of the partners! I refused to answer and quickly gave the phone to Gamil to handle. This was so frustrating for me that I spoke a few expletives. A discriminatory remark posed at me by an Arab in my own country and in my own business! So this is how it feels to be discriminated against.

CHAPTER 8

Post Euphoria

Relatively excited and happy about our business Gamil continued to create and formulate programs on a day-by-day basis. I continued my work at Lehman Brothers and went to the station after work to see what was going on. I was needed there to help out with the time sheets, the payroll, and wrote letters as necessary. Gamil ran around the office, checking in on the editors and making sure that all was going smoothly.

Thus began an exhausting time for me. My demanding and intense job at Lehman began at 8:00 a.m. and ended at about 6:30 p.m. each day. Then I would walk down to Exchange Place to look in on the station. We usually left at 11:00 p.m. and arrived home by midnight. On a few days during the week, I didn't make supper; it was too late, and I had to get up early the next day for work. Besides, I was exhausted.

Sometimes Gamil would get upset with me because of this. He even complained to his mother, who asked him "What do you want your wife to do? She has a full time job and is helping you out at the station; she has no time to cook." She volunteered to make him several dinners so that he could put them in our refrigerator and have it available to eat. Gamil was happy with this arrangement; he had his home-cooked meals ready and waiting for him when he got home. The pressure was off me.

As I was preparing the second bi-weekly payroll for ten people and bringing the balance in the checkbook forward, I realized that we had just enough funds to continue for one more week. I couldn't believe it! I rechecked the numbers, and it was true. The Social Security payments and payroll taxes were eating away at our funds. We had paid for much of the equipment and installations with cash. I told Gamil, and he was very nervous about the news. He wondered what I had done wrong. "What I had done wrong? Really!" I had told him that the six hundred thousand dollars would not be enough to start. He wanted to know if we could stop paying the payroll taxes and asked our accountant if that was possible. One of the partners, who was present when I told Gamil this news, said, "This is what happens in business. You will have problems and you must determine how to remedy them."

What had happened? I realized that we hadn't collected any accounts receivable yet for the advertising contracts we had entered into. I suggested to Gamil that we start calling people to collect the money and get it into the company so we could build the balance in the checking account.

So we started calling the customers. I didn't make any of the calls since they really didn't trust an American on the phone. So Gamil had his receptionist/secretary make some of the calls, and he made others. They found that the customers expected us to visit them at their places of businesses, have a cup of tea, engage in conversation, and collect the money.

"What?" I exclaimed. "Haven't they heard of the post office?"

Gamil said, "This is what they do in Egypt. A bill collector visits each customer and collects the money."

"But this is not Egypt!" I replied. No wonder our cash flow was so poor; no one was paying, let alone paying on time.

I examined our policy on writing advertising contracts. We weren't taking a deposit on the contract and were letting the customers pay monthly. We trusted these people to pay us according to the contract, but they weren't. This was a bad way to do business. No wonder we had no money. Nothing was being collected initially from sales!

We got smarter about writing our contracts and billing. We took a down payment of 20 per cent on the contracts, and installments had to be paid in advance. I contracted with Dun & Bradstreet for their small business collection services, including the ability to check the credit rating of each new customer who came to us. Before we accepted a new customer, we checked out his or her credit rating. This was a sounder way of doing business. With all my learning in undergraduate and graduate schools, I hadn't realized what cash flow really meant and the difference between cash flow and profits.

But our cash flow problems became more serious because we were two months into our business when we woke up. We didn't have enough to pay our monthly bills -- rent, transmission fees, and payroll. Gamil made the decision to ask the partners to put more money into the company so that we could continue. Imagine you are the head of a company and have to ask your partners for more money to continue after just starting. Gamil was so embarrassed and nervous. He called the partners in, told them of the situation, and asked for more money. Only four partners out of seven put in more money. But it was in the form of a loan to the partnership.

We got forty thousand dollars to continue, but that still wasn't enough. Gamil decided to give up his salary to continue the business. Of course, I wasn't being paid for what I did there; I worked to help my husband. And he was comfortable knowing that I would be supporting the household without his salary for the short term.

I also nagged him to hire a full-time salesman to go out into the community to bring in more sales. For a television station, advertising sales are critical to the operation and should be the largest percentage of revenues. We also had money coming from the cable companies for our share of the revenue from cable subscribers, but this would come forty-five days after our services were provided to our subscribers -- another timing delay in the receipt of fees for our services.

The advertising salesman was doing a fine job and one of the partners was assisting in getting contracts. But we needed more. We needed better clients than merchants and professionals in the area. I got hold of the Red Book of advertising agents who represent companies and place ads on television. I got one of the American-speaking assistants, Huda, to call buyers who had relationships with Arabic companies, like the airlines, to develop a relationship with them.

We learned that the budgets for advertising were developed in the fall for the following year and that we had to get on their radar screen at that time. So we did. Huda and I prepared a presentation kit, sent it off to various advertising companies, and followed up for questions and indications of interest. She signed contracts with Ford, Emirates Air, Royal Air Maroc, and Egypt Air. Even with these higher-level clients, we learned that Egypt Air wanted to barter with us in the form of tickets. Well, that was acceptable, since Gamil would travel overseas, but we didn't want this to be universal since you can't pay all your bills with barter; we needed cash.

We soon realized that cash was not going to be our only problem. A director of a movie that we had aired demanded thirty thousand dollars in royalty fees. We indicated that we had exclusive rights for the movie and the station did not owe him anything. He said that we didn't get the rights from him. We were puzzled.

We contacted an entertainment and media attorney, described the situation, and asked what we should do? He said that royalties and copyrights on films made overseas and aired in the United States were not enforceable in the United States. We were protected but that didn't stop enterprising people who would call and demand the payment. We then wondered how exclusive some of our contracts really were. We realized that there was no such thing as "exclusivity" when dealing with distributors in the Middle East. Television stations in the Middle East showed the programs we had. We spent over one hundred thousand dollars on an exclusive contract with a distributor in the Middle East, and it wasn't valid. That was a hard lesson to learn.

About eight months after we started broadcasting in April, we learned that an Arabic television station out of Washington, D.C. had started up in December 1991. It was called ANA (Arab-Net) and was run by a Saudi national. This station was delivered via satellite (direct-to-home) and was able to go nationwide among viewers who had a satellite dish to receive the signal. Of course, Gamil was upset after learning this. And the Saudi owner had enough money to build his business without the need to raise funding.

We met with the owner of this television station in an effort to learn more about his operation and to see if we could form a partnership with regard to sharing programming. This worked out well for a while, but ANA was later purchased by MBC (Middle East Broadcasting Corporation) out of Dubai in 1994; the management at ANA changed, and our relationship cooled.

To alleviate his fears about the business, I reminded Gamil that we had a franchise for Arabic television in the New York/New Jersey metropolitan area. We held the distribution in this significant area, something that would be valuable to other Arabic television stations looking to expand into the United States. We had greater saturation into Arabic homes reaching over one hundred thousand households than the potential for other areas of the country with smaller populations of Arabic-speaking people. This thought gave him some comfort about the business. It was estimated that the total market in the United States of Arabic-speaking people was three million. Without the concentration that we had, it would be difficult for other television companies to make money here.

Two years after we started, I was checking our statistics from the three cable companies we contracted with as I usually did and noticed that the numbers for US Cable of Patterson were going down. I inquired as to the reason for this decline and the subsequent decline of our fees for this franchise. I learned that the Arab customers were splicing the cables in the buildings to share the television broadcast with their neighboring tenants. There would be only one customer on record in the building. If there was a retail business on the ground floor, the proprietor would splice the cable and share it with the tenants.

This was crazy! I would think that the cable company would police this and remedy the situation. I was told that they didn't have the resources to do it; they were a small company, and they too were losing money on this. We were flabbergasted. They couldn't police and protect their equipment? We were losing money by transmitting our signal to them; the link cost more than the fees we were earning. This link was a losing proposition for us. In the next few months the numbers went down more, and the cable company decided to pull our service. So we eliminated the link to Patterson.

CHAPTER 9

The World Trade Center Bombing, 1993

On February 26, 1993, New York City experienced its first terrorist bombing. At approximately 12:18 p.m., a van entered the parking garage of the North Tower of the World Trade Center. Shortly after, there was a huge explosion that tore into the basement of the building and created a crater more than sixty feet wide and collapsed several concrete floors. It killed six people and injured a thousand others, and many in the building suffered smoke inhalation.

After a massive manhunt conducted by the FBI and New York City officials, Mohammed Salameh, Ahmad Ajaj, Nidal Ayyad and Mahmoud Abouhalima were captured within days and later convicted and sentenced to life in prison in 1994.

The mastermind of the attack, Ramzi Ahmed Yousef, remained at large until February 1995, when he was arrested in Pakistan. He had been in the Philippines, and in a computer he left were terrorist plans that included a plot to kill Pope John Paul II and a plan to bomb fifteen American airliners in forty-eight hours. On the flight back to the United States, Yousef reportedly admitted to a Secret Service agent that he had directed the Trade Center attack from the beginning and even claimed to have set the fuse that exploded the 1,200-pound bomb. His only regret, the agent quoted Yousef saying, was that the 110-story tower did not collapse into its twin as planned -- a catastrophe that would have caused thousands of deaths.

Eyad Ismoil, who drove the Ryder van into the parking garage below the World Trade Center, was captured in Jordan that year and taken back to New York. All the men implicated had ties to Sheikh Omar Abdel Rahman, a radical Egyptian religious leader who operated out of Jersey City just across the Hudson River from Manhattan. In 1995, Rahman and ten followers were convicted of conspiring to blow up the United Nations headquarters and other New York landmarks. Prosecutors argued that the World Trade Center attack was part of that conspiracy, though little clear evidence of this charge was presented.[1]

Lehman Brothers was in the World Financial Center across Church Street from the World Trade Center. Although I didn't hear the bomb go off because of my location in the building, my colleagues on the other side of the building had a front-row seat overlooking the parking garage. It was awful. Black smoke was billowing out of the garage from the lower levels. Workers in the building were being evacuated from the tower, and all had to walk down from their floors, which took several hours from the highest floors. Some were able to leave on their own, and many others were assisted by co-workers or by firefighters. All were covered with soot, their faces blackened by the smoke. Many were having difficulty breathing.

The Winter Garden, the beautiful, glass-enclosed plaza near the marina on the Hudson River, decorated with palm trees and containing retail shops, was transformed into a triage area for the victims of the bombing. It was a terrible sight. Victims were laying on floors in the space and were given oxygen and medical aid.

---

1   "World Trade Center bombed," History.com, http://www.history.com/this-day-in-history/world-trade-center-bombed.

I related this information to Gamil who was hearing about the bombing from the Associated Press news feed at the station. He couldn't believe it. I said that it might have been executed by Arab terrorists, and he replied, "A Muslim would not do this!"

After this event, I realized that the bombing had a profound effect on me. Whenever I was asked what company I started with my husband, I was ashamed to answer with the name of the television station. I was concerned that people would look at me in a different way, as if I were a friend of the enemy. I would merely answer that it was an ethnic television station covering the New York/New Jersey area. I no longer was able to state proudly that my business was The Arabic Channel and that I had helped create it.

Shortly after the attack on the World Trade Center, the FBI visited us. They wanted to know if we had been contacted by anyone involved in the bombing. They wanted to be made aware of anyone who contacted The Arabic Channel who was remotely involved with the terrorists who were arrested or who knew any of the terrorists. They also indicated that they would tap our phones and would be listening for any contact.

You can imagine how we felt. One, we didn't realize that the FBI or any governmental agency was aware that The Arabic Channel existed. And two, every time we picked up the phone we had to be careful of what we said so as not to cause the authorities any concern. Of course, we had to convey this message to our staff in a way that wouldn't raise any concerns or suspicions, and hope that they would comply with our instructions.

About two months later, Gamil received a phone call from William Kunstler and Ron Kuby, the attorneys representing Sheikh Omar Abdel-Rahman, the blind cleric, who was head of the Egyptian-based terrorist group Gama'a al-Islamiyah, responsible for the 1993 World Trade Center bombing. They visited us at our offices just four blocks from the World Trade Center and wanted The Arabic Channel to portray the sheikh as a peaceful person who preached love and respect for all peoples in a documentary to be created and aired by The Arabic Channel. They said that especially since he was blind, he could not possibly conceive of such plans to cause such destruction; he was innocent.

You can imagine Gamil's reaction to these visitors in light of the FBI visit. He politely declined this request, indicating that The Arabic Channel was apolitical and a good citizen of the United States. These men withdrew from our offices, and we never heard from them again. Whew! We were suddenly becoming well-known by the American and Arabic communities and governmental agencies! As he had promised, Gamil contacted the FBI and told them of this encounter.

CHAPTER 10

Partnering Pays Off

We were constantly thinking of ways to increase our revenue. I had seen a program on public access television that was exclaimed as being part of the station's leased-time effort for the community. Bingo! That could be an answer for us. We could lease time to local producers of programs and charge a fee. I mentioned this to Gamil and encouraged him by saying, "Let's do this." It seemed promising.

But we needed the permission of Time Warner, since our contract said they would have to approve of any deviation from Arabic language programming. Gamil called the marketing director at Time Warner and told him of our plans. To our surprise he said that he was getting calls from local producers to air their programs, but they couldn't conceive of how to incorporate those programs into their busy programming lineups. We were the answer.

Time Warner referred us to these programmers, and we set aside Saturday mornings as the time for them to present their programs. This was a great way for us to earn additional revenue and become known to another ethnic community, the Guyanese. We now had a third revenue stream to support our operations.

Later, I received a call from a media buyer who wondered if we would be interested in airing showmercials, those thirty minute programs you watch for ten minutes before realizing you're watching a commercial selling a product. If we aired the programs and if a viewer using our dedicated 800 number called in to order the product, we would receive a commission for the sale. "Of course, we were interested." We could air these programs late at night to capture people who couldn't sleep. Now we had a fourth revenue stream to assist in the station's survival. We could receive commissions anywhere from three hundred to $1,200 a month depending on the quality of the products being offered.

Our Arabic customer base was upset with our airing showmercials. "What is this? This is not our Arabic programs. There can be nothing other than Arabic language on *our* station," the Arabic viewers told us. If we told them that this was a way for us to make money to support the station, some of them didn't care. But they still indicated ownership of the station by saying "*our* station". Had we created customer loyalty?

CHAPTER 11

Enter the Competition - Satellite Stations

Our position in the United States as the only privately-owned, Arabic-language television station in the United States running twenty-four hours a day, seven days a week would be shortly outlived. Changes in technology from analog to digital and the need of satellite stations to reach more viewers, would put us on edge.

In 1994 we received a call from Michael Kelly, president of Kelly Broadcasting Service out of Orange, New Jersey. He wanted to meet with us to learn more about us. Gamil called one of the partners and me to attend this meeting. Kelly introduced himself as a distributor of foreign-language programming and owned a satellite facility in Orange that assisted foreign satellite stations in reaching the United States. He carried Dubai Television and other European stations.

He wanted to purchase us for around three million dollars so that he could expand his distribution into the systems we were on. By doing so, he would have the viewership of The Arabic Channel, which was about 250,000 households. Earlier I had discussed with Gamil that the only reason someone would want to purchase our channel was for its distribution network, which we held the

contracts for. This would allow for immediate expansion. A potential buyer wouldn't be interested in our studio or the programs
we held the rights to. And I was right. To Kelly Broadcasting we
were valuable for our distribution network.

Our partners felt that a company that was now about four years
old should demand more money. We wanted at least five million
to surrender our business because of the investment of time and
money we had put into it. Kelly would not hear of it and reiterated
his prior offer. We refused, and Kelly stormed out of our offices.
Later we learned that Kelly had gone directly to Time Warner and
threatened to sue them if they didn't honor his offer of buying a
channel on their system. Time Warner considered this threat ridiculous and frivolous.

With the advancement of broadcast technology other satellite stations entered our broadcast space in 1995. The opportunities for
them to gain viewers and popularity were great, and they had the
money to invade the United States. I couldn't understand how these
satellite stations could make money here. Again, the estimated
size of the Arabic speaking population in the United States was
approximately three million people; that is a very small market for
so many satellite companies. However, moneyed Saudi Sheikhs
owned these satellite stations: ART (Arab Radio and Television),
MBC (Middle East Broadcast Company), Dubai Television, and
Nile TV. Along with this invasion, many companies sold satellite
dishes to potential viewers so that they could receive signals in their
homes and enjoy the programming. These distribution companies
competed for viewers and duplicated the television programming.
Potential viewers were often confused by these offers.

In 1998 the Dish Network made contracts with the Middle Eastern
satellite station companies and offered potential viewers various
bundled packages of Arabic television programs at various prices.
This event put the earlier established distribution companies out
of business and caused Kelly Broadcasting a headache.

In 2000 EchoStar, a direct-to-home satellite company owned by the Dish Network, purchased Kelly Broadcasting for three million in cash and stock. Kelly became a senior vice president of international programming and operations for them. He had made a great deal for himself.

We were watching these events to determine our plan of defense. We had to offer our current viewers the best programs we could find. We also needed Time Warner's help with marketing to keep our viewers loyal.

For customers to receive these satellite stations, they had to purchase a dish receiver and mount it on their building. Many of the Arabic speaking people lived in multi-unit dwellings, and the landlords wouldn't allow tenants to mount a satellite dish outside their apartment or on the roof of the building. We believed this restriction was in our favor because it would limit the growth of the satellite stations.

Time Warner responded by adding us to its affiliated companies in Staten Island, Manhattan, and North Manhattan. Now we could be seen by people in the United Nations, and in those colleges that offered Arabic language studies, such as, Columbia University and New York University, as well as the residents of those areas.

About this time, the effect of running this business was taking its toll on our marriage. There were many late nights. Dinners together didn't exist, because of commitments Gamil had late into the night. Sometimes I wouldn't see him for days. He would come home early in the morning, just when I left for work. We were like ships passing in the night. We would greet one another on the stairs, and then I would go to work and he would go to sleep.

We were not communicating about our personal lives or the events that occurred during our days. All we had to talk about and in common was the business. It was our baby. Our marriage was based on running a business and not running a marriage. I was feeling neglected while Gamil was out schmoozing with his Arab friends.

He tried to appease me by taking me on a trip to Cairo, the purpose of which was to attend meetings to arrange for some kind of business. On past trips, I stayed in the Cairo apartment and waited for his return in the evening. It wasn't fun! Television was in Arabic and was on during the day for about two to three hours, and then programming would resume in the evening. I couldn't go out, because I didn't know how to get around, let alone read the street signs or the names of the shops. And all the neighborhoods looked the same with their large buildings of French design.

The next time he asked me to go with him to Cairo I asked why he wanted me to go. He said, "Because you are my wife." I refused to go. He was shocked at this. So you can imagine what happened in time. We grew apart and ultimately the marriage fell apart. We were divorced in late 1997.

After our divorce, I stayed away from the station; even though I was a limited partner, I didn't want to confuse the employees by my being there. A few months after our divorce became final, Gamil remarried, which was a total shock to me. I felt like I had lost my best friend. But I eventually got over it.

About three months after Gamil remarried, he called me and asked that I come back to the station and work. He said that no one could do the job I had been doing for the station, and things were in a shambles. I lost my job at Lehman in late 1994 due to a reduction in the workforce and had gotten a job in a consulting firm. But I didn't like it there. I returned to the station working only part-time while looking for other work. Ultimately, I worked at the station full time. This freed Gamil to travel on business; there was someone at the office who knew how to manage it.

CHAPTER 12

The Desert Rose Tour

In the early spring of 2000, Miles Copeland, the promoter and agent for Sting, called and spoke to Gamil regarding the possibility of us promoting the Desert Rose Tour later in June. Copeland is heavily involved with Middle Eastern music. I later discovered that his father, also named Miles Copeland, was a CIA agent assigned to the Middle East, and his family lived there for many years. Miles has a great interest in the Middle East and even has a troupe of sophisticated belly dancers who go on tour there and here.

Sting's Brand New Day album was being released at that time featuring Cheb Mamy, a famous Rai singer from Algeria, singing the song, Desert Rose, with Sting. This was so exciting for us. Being in a relationship with Miles and Sting would draw the attention of both the Arabic and the American communities. There also was potential for additional promotions later on. I also had the great pleasure of meeting Sting and Miles in our offices.

We began by scheduling an interview with Mamy to broadcast on The Arabic Channel. We also showed both Mamy's and Sting's music videos to generate interest from our viewing public. We also had the Desert Rose music video, which we were to broadcast later in June.

Sting's interview was a little problematic. We had to have an English-speaking, Arabic interviewer who could research Sting's life, prepare an interview, and translate Sting's responses for our Arabic-speaking audience. Because of our cooperative effort with ANA, we arranged to have one of the best interviewers from ANA come to New York and interview Sting. We would then release the interview to be broadcast in New York and in the Washington, D.C. area on ANA's network.

The interview took place in our offices. We shared our floor with a law firm, and the women who worked there wanted to see Sting and have him autograph their albums. We coordinated this meeting so that when Sting arrived, the women from the law firm could come in and meet him. They came in all smiles, giggling and blushing. He was so gracious and calm while signing their albums; it was quite a contrast with the lack of composure from the visiting women.

In June, Sting made a televised appearance in the morning on NBC's *Today Show*. We were asked to come in, interview him again in the green room and then shoot the Desert Rose song performed by Sting, his band and Mamy outside on Rockefeller Center Plaza. There was such electricity in the air. There was a huge crowd gathered around the stage and in the streets, screaming and shouting for Sting to appear. Our cameraman was positioned near the stage, and he was told not to go beyond the barrier surrounding the stage. When Sting came out and started his song, the crowd quieted down to enjoy his music. Our cameraman was so excited to shoot such a great artist he proceeded to jump the barrier and get up on the stage to get a better shot of Sting. The band seemed alarmed by this move, but Sting ignored him and continued his song. The Rockefeller Center security guards emerged to get him off the stage. We thought he would be arrested, but he jumped off just in time to avoid any altercation.

Later in September, we interviewed and filmed Simon Shaheen and his band, Qantara, the opening act for Sting at the end of his Desert Rose tour at the Jones Beach Theatre in Long Island. Shaheen is a virtuoso composer and performer on both the violin and the oud, a Middle Eastern string instrument. He combines Middle Eastern sounds with contemporary jazz. Although well known in the Middle East, Shaheen's appearance with Sting high-lighted his abilities as a composer and musician as he began his own tour in the United States. It also illustrated Sting's interest and appreciation of all kinds of music.

CHAPTER 13

The Internet Craze

In the summer of 1999 there was much activity for web site formation and development of businesses using Internet technology. Many avenues were opening up for distributing products and sharing of information. I suggested to Gamil that we consider having a web site for our station on which we could provide our viewers with daily program listings and stories about various movie stars. We would have to think of what we could put on the web site and how to execute it. I have connections with to many graduate students at Polytechnic Institute where I taught global marketing. I could find out who would be interested in helping us build a website.

As was usual with Gamil, he took this idea and elaborated on it, suggesting we create a website containing various languages and providing the news, video clips of the shows we produced and sales of films, if we could get the license for the sales. It sounded like a great idea. However, Gamil wanted to hire a website de-signer and graphic artist to work on it. We asked for bids and settled on a company that completed the website in about two months.

I asked some of my students if they were interested in a part-time job. We knew that the website would require updating, and we wanted to add other material. So a student from PolyTech came in the evenings after his classes to work on some backend work and to teach us how to update the pages.

Gamil became so motivated by this project that he helped design several features of the web site. We decided to call it Ethnicnet because of the various languages it contained. We hired college students to build a mailing list from our lists of television viewers so that we could notify them about the new website. We also sold advertising on the website in conjunction with the television advertising.

When the site had been up about four months, we received a telephone call from Peter Palmer, a marketing vice president at EMI Music in London. He thought our website would be the perfect place to sell EMI international music. It amazed me that someone had found us in the world of the Internet and wanted to form a partnership with us in order to sell CDs.

The plan was to for EMI to build another website, called Ethnicnetmusic. We would own the name. We would market the website by placing ads in newspapers and on our television station. We could select the CDs that we thought our audience would be interested in and even suggest the pricing for the CDs, so that they would be attractive and competitive. This caused a flurry of activity in our offices and many phone calls from England to get the website ready. Gamil made several trips to London to meet the senior managers and build a relationship with them.

Finally, the website was launched and we began selling CDs.

About nine months after the website was launched Palmer was the victim of downsizing and left the organization. Another person was put in his place. We thought his replacement would come to Ethnicnetmusic and create more energy for the site, but he didn't have an interest in it; it wasn't on his agenda. Sales were not significant enough for him to further the project, and Ethnicnetmusic was eventually shut down. This was such a disappointment for us, but we were in the hands of a partner who had the product and didn't want to continue this venture.

As in all cases, there was something brewing at EMI Music. The company was being "shopped" to other recording companies. The industry had become very competitive, and it was difficult for EMI to make money without merging with another company. Its artists were not as popular as those on other record labels, such as Warner and Sony. So there was much dissention in the company. A few months after we closed the website, we saw managers leaving for other companies or developing their own enterprises.

Ethnicnet lasted for a couple more years, but as with other things Gamil lost interest, and we closed it down.

CHAPTER 14

A Wild Goose Chase

Early in March 2001, Gamil had a telephone conversation with someone in Egypt who told him that the government of Dubai was interested in investing in American companies in order to build an industrial park in Dubai. Dubai was offering American companies incentives to move there, including housing for the employees, no taxes on wages and corporate income generated in Dubai, and preferential tax rates for the corporate building. This person suggested Gamil visit Dubai to see what was going on, and perhaps he would be able to generate interest in The Arabic Channel and obtain an investment from the sheikhs in Dubai.

Of course, this was very enticing for Gamil. He wanted to go there, but he had a scheduling conflict and could not travel as far as Dubai. "So," he thought, "why not send Margo to do this?" He called me in and told me that he was sending me to Dubai. When I asked why, he told me that we may be able to get an investment from the Dubai government. I thought about this a moment. It certainly would be nice to get out of the office to visit a new and different land. But what was going on in Dubai that would interest Gamil so? And why wouldn't he go to discuss an investment in the business himself?

He merely explained that they were investing in American companies and thought why shouldn't we get in on it? I told him that

I would not go unless I had a male chaperone to escort me through-out my visit. It would be easier for me, and I would feel safer in such a different land. I remembered that when Gamil and I went to Egypt on our honeymoon, all the Egyptians stared at me we walked through Cairo. His mother walked with me with our arms entwined, and I thought, "Gee, is someone going to steal me?" They stared at my blond hair and blue eyes. It was a little scary.

So it was arranged. Gamil had his father meet me at the airport in Cairo, help me through customs, and then take me to the hotel where I would stay overnight. All the while, I was wondering if I was on a wild goose chase.

In the morning, my male chaperone, Mahmoud, arrived. We had breakfast together to get acquainted, and then we left for the air-port again, to travel to Dubai. It was such a long trip. I couldn't believe it. It took five hours to cross over Saudi Arabia, stop over in Bahrain and then arrive in Dubai. It was like taking a plane from New York to California.

The ride in from the airport revealed an ultra modern and highly developed city. The tall buildings were unique architecturally, and were made of glass that gleamed and sparkled in the Saudi sun. The majority of the cars on the road were Mercedes or BMWs, and all were driven by East Indian chauffeurs.

After checking in to our hotel, we agreed to would meet in the morning for breakfast and then leave for our meeting with the minister of economic development. At breakfast, Mahmoud in-troduced me to a journalist who had a relationship with the minis-ter of economic development and who would be joining us in the meeting. I wondered what his involvement was, and I would soon find out.

We went to an area under development that looked like an in-dustrial park. We drove by an area for housing, and I was told it was for the employees at the industrial park. There were rows of light-brown houses that looked Mexican. As we passed the industrial park there were buildings for Microsoft, Cisco, Symantec, and others were going up. We soon arrived at the administrative building for the industrial park. In a conference room shaped like a glass cylinder, we met the minister of economic development. I felt like I was in a fishbowl. We could see everyone outside the room, working at their desks and looking at the new arrivals. And we were looking back out at them.

The minister entered the room dressed in the white headdress and robe typical of Saudis. He introduced himself very graciously, and I introduced myself and told him about my employment at Lehman and my interest in The Arabic Channel. With his American accent, he mentioned that he was educated at Stamford. I had attended many meetings while I was at Lehman Brothers, but this one, sitting opposite a sheikh dressed the way he was, was so weird.

The journalist and my chaperone were quiet. The minister gave me his speech as to what was going on with the development, which we could see as we came in, and asked why I might be interested in moving the company there. I knew there was no chance of getting a direct investment from him in The Arabic Channel after hearing the classic economic development scenario, including its economic benefits and tax incentives.

I told him that what I saw was very beautiful, and the housing appeared to be very comfortable. I said we would be interested, and that I would return to New York and inform my partner of what I saw. I also asked if there was any possibility of the government investing separately in The Arabic Channel. At that moment, the journalist sat up and leaned forward, suddenly interested in the conversation. The minister said that Dubai was solely interested in developing the industrial park and inviting as many companies as possible. There would be no investment in a company per se. The journalist's face became clouded.

I ended the meeting with the minister who was very gracious to me and shook my hand very tenderly as if to flirt with me. There had certainly been a miscommunication or a misunderstanding between Gamil and the person he'd spoken to on the phone. And I had felt that I had wasted my time.

As we left the development, the journalist was very brusque and seemed annoyed. He said something in Arabic to my chaperone that I didn't understand. We dropped him off at his office and never saw him again. I knew that somehow he stood to gain if there were a deal with the minister, perhaps some kind of finder's fee. No wonder he was so annoyed! He had wasted his time and lost out on a fee.

I made plans to return to New York as quickly as possible. It was a very short trip to Dubai, taking just four days round trip. It almost felt like shuttle diplomacy.

CHAPTER 15

World Trade Center Tragedy, 2001

On the morning of September 11, 2001, I had an appointment for an interview at a search firm in the World Trade Center at 9:30 a.m. Originally, the appointment was for 8:30 a.m., but I asked that it be made later. There I was in the subway, making my way down to Lower Manhattan for my interview, when the conductor announced that there was a police action at Cortlandt Street and we would be delayed. "Oh great! Just when I have an important interview," I said under my breath.

When the train pulled into the Union Square station I immediately transferred to the 4 train which would take me toward the World Trade Center as well, but only a block closer. While I was on that crowded train, someone came and said to the passengers, "Did you hear what happened? A plane crashed into one of the towers of the World Trade Center." Someone asked which one? He didn't know. While he had been in a diner eating his breakfast, the announcement had come across a televised news program about the plane crashing into the tower, and he wanted to come down and see it for himself.

A woman standing directly behind me said to me, "I hope it isn't in the building I work in". I asked her where she worked, and she said in the north tower. She asked my help with directions at Cortlandt Street, since she wasn't sure where this train would take her. Well, the train didn't stop at Cortlandt Street; we rode right past it as the conductor announced that Wall Street would be the next stop.

We left the subway and arrived at street level by Trinity Church. I looked up at the twin towers, and the sight was surreal. They looked like two huge candles burning in the beautiful fall air. The area was eerily quiet, even though many people were walking around. They were dazed. Men helped women who were crying and walking shoeless. Some people sat on the curbs near the New York Stock Exchange, crying and dazed. Some were bleed- ing. There was litter flying around, and I realized that some of it was airline tickets and singed newspapers. I saw luggage strewn about, shoes and handbags.

As I walked toward Pine Street, I realized that my interview was surely off, and the woman who was accompanying me was aghast at what she was seeing. I told her that she should get back on the subway and make her way quickly to her home in Connecticut. But she didn't have a token. I gave her one and wished her luck in arriving at her destination.

I turned down Pine Street and made my way to my office. I knew that the early staff would be there and probably would be waiting for instructions as to what to do. As I walked toward Exchange Place, people were hurriedly leaving their offices. They were afraid that another plane would target one of the many tall buildings in that area. A crowd had gathered in Chase Manhattan Plaza, and someone was calling names of employees from a roster. People were leaving 20 Exchange Place while I was entering it.

As I opened the door to my offices, I saw that our receptionist was crying, and our engineer told me we had to leave the building. It was too dangerous to remain in the building so high up. They were very anxious. He then led me into the studio and showed me that he had been filming the towers by leaning out of the window with the camera. They told me that they had phoned Gamil earlier and told him of the incident. But not realizing the full impact of what they were telling him, Gamil told them they had to remain there and work the station. Of course, I didn't agree.

I told the staff to close the office, put a tape on air which showed our logo and color bars, and let that run. I knew that if the tape ran out, the video player would capture the last frame and broadcast that until someone removed the tape. I turned to the Associated Press news station and read that another plane had indeed crashed into the Pentagon. "What was happening?" I asked myself.

I heard screams from the hall and went outside to see what was going on. The women from the law firm next door were on the fire escape looking at the fire at the towers. They screamed as they witnessed people jumping from them. I saw that the south tower had a bulge in it right under the flames, and I knew that its fall was imminent.

Ten minutes later, just as I was locking the door for us to leave, my engineer said "Look at the window!" I looked up and saw that it had become night; the view was completely black. The sky had become dark and foreboding. The first tower had fallen.

We made it down to the lobby and gathered there with other tenants of the building. No one could go out; it was too dangerous. We could not see across the narrow street, as debris fell down in the darkness. We heard someone who was listening on his portable radio say that the second tower had fallen.

We stayed there about half an hour more and saw some people entering the building completely covered in ash. It was a wonder they could make it to the building. My receptionist was anxious and insisted that we leave. But how? Outside you couldn't see your hand in front of you; it was too dangerous.

Several minutes later, a person from the Fire Department spoke on the building's public address system. He told us that we had to evacuate Lower Manhattan and start walking east toward the river. The building management gave us water and masks to cover our faces, and we proceeded east down Wall Street to the river.

All you could see was the drizzle of falling ash. We walked in gray ash that was about four inches deep. All I could think was, "Who am I stepping on?" We were soon covered in ash. We made it down to the East River and I saw small boats and ferries coming up to the Wall Street Pier to evacuate people. Some of the boats were going to Jersey City, and the Atlantic Highlands, and others to Brooklyn. We got on the boat to Brooklyn.

As we sat there crossing the East River, we could see the rising black smoke from the World Trade Center. All of the passengers stared back at it in silence. Some cried. Others were in shock. It was then that I realized we were at war.

Once we arrived in Brooklyn, we took busses and made our way home.

Gamil and I were concerned about the station. Was there any damage to the equipment from all the dust or to our space? We were not broadcasting except for the color bars. We were concerned that we might breach our contract with Time Warner. Gamil had to get in to examine the station. But we were not permitted to enter the area. No one could enter Lower Manhattan unless they lived there. There were police barricades along Canal Street and there was heavy security. We couldn't enter the area for five days. Subways were terminating at Prince Street from uptown or not even entering Whitehall from Brooklyn.

Time Warner contacted Gamil and told him that we had to be up and running. But we needed their assistance to get us back in. Time Warner called the mayor's office and they gave us permission to enter our building. Armed National Guard soldiers were stationed at each corner in Lower Manhattan, and we had to identify ourselves at each post.

We checked our premises and found that the telephone line for the Associated Press feed was cut as were other lines in the building. Our line went to the Telephone Building across from the World Trade Center on Vesey Street. A portion of the tower that fell had narrowly missed the Telephone Building, but lines were cut underneath the World Trade Center. Our main telephone system was not affected since we used another carrier, Teligent, for our phones. Later other tenants in the building asked to use our phones to contact their telephone companies or contact clients; we were glad to help them.

The building management had taken extra precautions about filtering the air in. They had shut down the air-conditioning as soon as the tragedy occurred. The foul smell from the World Trade Center site was overwhelming, but in the building, all was fine.

Nothing happened to the broadcast transmission. At this time we were using fiber optic cable for transmission which ran in the ground and not by microwave. The underground cables were not affected by the attack.

I remember Gamil saying about the attacks, "Not again. Everyone will blame the Arabs for this one too." He was very upset that there would be increased discrimination against Arab peoples. Al Qaeda came into the picture, and once again it was proved that the people who flew the planes into the towers were acting on the orders of Osama Bin Laden, who was also linked to the garage bombing of the World Trade Center.

And how did this event impact The Arabic Channel? Our advertising business that had been good was now nonexistent. It was as though Arabs disappeared from the business scene and put their heads in the sand. No one wanted to draw attention to themselves, let alone advertise their businesses. Our advertising earnings dropped dramatically by approximately 75 percent.

We were really struggling this time. But we weren't the only ones. Many of the businesses in the area weren't able to function because of the clean up being conducted at the WTC site. People were so depressed that they didn't want to come down to Lower Manhattan. Businesses were leaving the area for other locations uptown which they felt were safer than the Wall Street area. The city, state and federal governments had to do something to assist the businesses in the area and stabilize it.

Much of the bitter feeling toward Arabic people could have been mitigated, I believe, if the imams had come out strongly against the terrorists by saying that they deplored what had happened and that Arabs are peace-loving peoples. They should have said that terrorism is not encouraged by the Quran, and that the Quran teaches peace and love. But they didn't say anything and did nothing to quell the fears of the American people and the Arabic people.

Luckily, we were able to take advantage of some of the programs that the federal government put into place to help businesses in the Ground Zero area reestablish. Loan programs and grants were applied for and won by many of the businesses. Landlords offered their vacated space at low rates. But overall, the atmosphere in the area was gray and depressing. It would take ten years to recover from the shock of the attacks.

To diminish discrimination against Arabic people and foster an understanding of the Muslim religion, the Parish of Trinity Church in New York City entered into an agreement with us in November 2001 to broadcast a program they created, entitled "Fundamentalism and Violence: A Dialogue Among Jewish, Christian and Muslim

Leaders," in an effort to help people understand and to see the similarities among the religions. Appearing in this program filmed at Columbia University was Karen Armstrong, the author of many books about religion, especially Islam, and Imam Feisal Abdul Rauf, who in 2010 would found the controversial Ground Zero mosque. The Arabic Channel aired this program in two parts and received much praise and criticism from our audience.

CHAPTER 16

Loss of Comcast Cablevision of Jersey City

In 2005 we suffered another blow to our business. Arabic Radio & Television (ART), made a deal with Comcast Cablevision of Jersey City offering to pay them two million dollars for a channel to show their movies and programs. As all cable television systems are constantly looking for ways to increase their revenue, they agreed. They put ART on a premier tier, which customers had to pay extra for.

While this deal was transpiring, our television programs kept going off the air and then coming back on again in the Jersey City area. It was as if someone were playing with the switch, turning the lights on and off. We complained to the operations people at Comcast unaware that ART was negotiating with them. We later believed the problems were a ploy by Comcast to get our viewers to switch to ART. Of course, we couldn't prove it. We were so upset, and our viewers were equally upset with this situation. But there was nothing we could do. Comcast Cablevision didn't want two Arabic television channels broadcasting on their system to their small market at the same time.

The realization that our small television station that started in 1991 was in danger of failing was defeating. We had no recourse but to reduce our expenses, cut staff, and manage our business as best we could. Gamil went on a tour of several satellite stations in the Middle East requesting that they consider expansion to the United States, with The Arabic Channel helping to open doors and manage their programming to be received in New York. But they weren't interested.

Then along came the Dish Network in the 2003, which expanded their channel capacity through digital technology and could well afford to have new stations included in their program lineup. They were able to add Nile TV, Future TV, Al Jazzera, Sudan TV, Yemen TV, Algeria TV, Morocco TV and several others.

CHAPTER 17

Loss of Focus

O f course, this news of strong competition coming in and the Arabic population wanting to see programs provided by the wealthy Saudis was also deflating. Gamil no longer wanted to compete with them and was thinking of ways to support The Arabic Channel. He believed that advertising would decline further. He envisioned Time Warner losing many of its viewers, who would rather watch the Dish Network programs. He wanted to maintain The Arabic Channel with revenues from another business – one located in Egypt.

Gamil began travelling several times a year to Cairo and investigating potential business there. He lost interest in The Arabic Channel, and I wanted him to close it down if he wanted to be an absentee owner, since managing the Arab employees was difficult for me; they wouldn't take instruction from a woman. He thought that I should run the station in his absence while he established a business in Cairo, but I refused.

This back and forth continued as Gamil tried to enter into several partnerships with Egyptians outside of the entertainment business. The potential partners were interested in his proposals, but when it came time to put the money on the table, they walked away. They would put sweat equity in, but not money. He told me that what interested him was acting as an agent; he wanted to pursue doing deals. I doubted that he had the connections for this type of business, but he said he did.

I lost interest in the business and hated to see it linger. I wanted out completely, and I told Gamil that I would retire soon. I continue to look at the books and the receipts, but only as a limited partner. Gamil continues to pursue rainbows overseas while keeping his finger on The Arabic Channel. When it will all end is only a matter of time, unless a miracle happens.

CHAPTER 18

An Opportunity Presents Itself, 2011

Technology created by Steve Jobs and Apple has created a revolution in the entertainment business. People are now able to view shows, play games, and talk to and text one another. This has led to the ability to see television via the Internet on your phone or other mobile device. Internet companies are looking for content to offer customers so they can see programs from anywhere, with digital broadband called IPTV (Internet Protocol TV). Television pictures are clearer, with an Internet cable connection. And television programs produced here in the United States can be made available through the Internet, making programming global. Anyone can see any program anywhere at any time. This is much cheaper to run; you don't need satellite transmissions or fiber optic cable transmission uplinking to satellites.

Gamil has been contacted by several IPTV companies to provide content to them so they can add us to their program lineup. He has become energized again and is working with a few IPTV companies to develop offerings for their systems. So there's hope for The Arabic Channel and communication to the world.

Will The Arabic Channel be able to revive itself? I don't know. Will Gamil be able to make it profitable again and be able to sell it to another company? I don't know.

But *Insha'Allah,* by the will of Allah, Gamil will do it!

INDEX

ABOUT THE AUTHOR

Marguerite M. Moore, an experienced strategy and financial professional and business consultant, is the co-founder of The Arabic Channel, the first Arabic language television channel seen in the United States. Through her efforts she has grown the channel to reach over 1,250,000 households in the New York/New Jersey metropolitan area.

Ms. Moore's business experience includes over ten years at Lehman Brothers Investment Bank as vice president of business development where she marketed the firm's investment banking business to CEOs and senior managers of middle market companies.

As an adjunct assistant professor at New York's Fashion Institute of Technology, Ms. Moore teaches entrepreneurship at the undergraduate level. Under the Design Entrepreneurs NYC program awarded to FIT by the NYC Economic Development Corporation, as part of the Fashion 2020 effort announced by Mayor Bloomberg in 2012, Ms. Moore instructed fashion designers admitted to the program and mentored several designers to perfect their business plans and strategies.

Prior to joining FIT, Ms. Moore was an adjunct professor at Polytechnic Institute in Brooklyn teaching marketing management at the graduate level. Ms. Moore holds an MBA in Finance and a BBA in Accounting from Pace University. Ms. Moore has written instructional modules and manuals on investment banking.